UQ COURSE FOR VISIONARY LEADERS

Lesson 7: Conscious Action and Lasting Results

Katia Doria Fonseca Vasconcelos

Dedication

It is with a deep sense of gratitude that we embark on this journey, sharing enriching perspectives and transformative experiences with each and every one of you, esteemed readers.

This volume, titled "UQ COURSE FOR VISIONARY LEADERS - Lesson 7: Conscious Action and Lasting Results," is more than a collection of printed words; it is an invitation to deepen our understanding, challenge our thinking, and embrace change through conscious action, guided by the principles of UQ.

I sincerely hope that this book becomes an inspiring source of knowledge and wisdom, empowering visionary leaders like yourselves to tread a path of continuous learning and innovation with UQ and AI as foundational pillars for a future of excellence and lasting achievements.

Our journey is shaped by a fervent dedication to the balance between technology and personal development. With every page, every chapter, we aspire to ignite an unwavering pursuit of growth, ongoing refinement, and wise and empathetic leadership in a ever-evolving world.

May this book be more than a reading, but a call to conscious action, deep introspection, and lasting transformation. May each concept explored here be a beacon that lights your path towards a new level of excellence.

I sincerely thank you for accompanying us on this journey of discovery and learning. May our collective efforts guide us beyond the familiar, propelling us toward a future filled with meaningful achievements and results that will resonate through time.

With gratitude and enthusiasm,

Katia Doria Fonseca Vasconcelos

Qu Course for Visionary Leaders

INTRODUCTION

Welcome to the exciting journey of Lesson 7 of the 'UQ COURSE FOR VISIONARY LEADERS', where we will delve into a fundamental theme for those who seek not only success, but also deep and lasting fulfillment in their lives and leadership. In this stage of our journey, we will immerse ourselves in the transformative power of 'Conscious Action' and its influence on achieving 'Lasting Results'.

Have you ever heard of the expression 'living on autopilot'? Often, we find ourselves in a frantic rhythm, carrying out tasks without deeply considering what we are doing or why we are doing it. However, true excellence, accomplishment, and lasting impact are intrinsically tied to our ability to act with consciousness, to make decisions aligned with our values, and to invest our time and energy in directions that truly matter.

Conscious action is more than just

performing tasks attentively; it involves a deep connection with our motivations, goals, and inner values. When we act consciously, we are cultivating a way of being in the world that allows us to observe our thoughts, feelings, and actions from a broader perspective. In this way, we gain the clarity needed to make choices that align with our deeper vision and aspirations.

On this journey, we will explore how conscious action intertwines with the principles of the UQ Concept (Universal Synchronic Intelligence Quotient) that have been the foundation of our course. We will understand how UQ strategies can be practically and tangibly applied to strengthen our ability to act consciously and, thus, unlock truly lasting results.

Throughout the upcoming sections, we will dive into the various dimensions of conscious action. We will discuss how this approach can influence our decisions, our productivity, our authenticity as leaders, and how we can apply it in different areas of our lives. Furthermore, we will explore resilience and continuous learning as essential pillars to sustain a journey of conscious action and lasting results.

Remember, conscious action is not a fixed state but a continuous process of self-discovery and evolution. It is a journey that challenges us to question, reflect, and grow constantly. By the end of this lesson, you will be equipped with practical tools and profound insights to cultivate conscious action in your role as a visionary leader and in all facets of your life.

Are you ready to explore the power of conscious action and its ability to create enduring results? Let's embark on this journey together and discover how we can balance our pursuit of success with a more conscious and meaningful approach. I am excited to guide you on this transformative path. Let's begin!

Table of Contents

Understanding UQ Principles
Recapping the UQ Concept

Human success is driven by the balance of UQ (Universal Synchronic Intelligence Quotient), a concept backed by scientific research and case studies. Numerous studies have explored the aspects of UQ and its effects in various areas of human life, providing concrete evidence of the relevance of this concept.

A study conducted by researchers at Stanford University revealed the importance of developing resilience and emotional control in achieving positive outcomes in careers and relationships. This research demonstrated how the ability to deal with adversities and control emotions contributes to making sound decisions and building healthy and productive relationships.

Renowned Harvard Business School professor Clayton Christensen highlights that disruptive innovation requires a change in approach and the overcoming of outdated paradigms. He emphasizes that success lies in embracing change and adapting quickly to new circumstances, underscoring the importance of adaptability in a constantly evolving world.

Psychologist and Nobel Prize-winning economist Daniel Kahneman reminds us that our decisions are influenced by how we perceive problems. By adopting a positive perspective and viewing challenges as learning opportunities, we can make better decisions and achieve superior outcomes. The theory of emotional intelligence, developed by Daniel Goleman, also aligns with the UQ concept, emphasizing the importance of emotional balance for personal and professional success.

Renowned psychologist and Harvard Graduate School of Education professor

Howard Gardner emphasizes the importance of balancing and developing all of our intelligences. He encourages us to reprogram our educational approach, valuing not only logical-mathematical intelligence but also emotional, musical, spatial, and other intelligences, enabling us to explore our full potential and embrace a 360-degree vision of situations.

The UQ concept, Universal Synchronic Intelligence Quotient, was conceived by renowned researcher and coach Katia Doria Fonseca Vasconcelos. It's an approach aimed at enhancing intelligence and cognitive skills through balancing the principles of 360-degree vision, Adaptability, Resilience, Synchronicity, and Emotional Control.

UQ was developed based on scientific foundations that prove the importance of balancing these principles in personal and professional development. Studies conducted by renowned researchers like psychologists Daniel Goleman and Daniel Kahneman highlight the relevance of emotional control and a positive perspective in making sound decisions and achieving personal success.

The application of UQ as a metric and benchmark occurs through evaluating and monitoring the UQ principles in different areas of life. Self-assessment is a fundamental tool in this process, allowing individuals to identify which principles they need to develop and balance to reach a higher level of intelligence and cognitive performance.

Balancing the potentials of UQ is essential for tackling complex challenges. By balancing 360-degree vision, Adaptability, Resilience, Synchronicity, and Emotional Control, the chances of finding effective solutions to problems increase significantly. This approach provides a broad and comprehensive view of challenges, allowing them to be faced with confidence, creativity, and effectiveness.

Developing potentials and achieving balance in UQ requires dedication, practice, and continuous self-development. It's a process that involves personal commitment to enhancing cognitive and emotional skills, as well as seeking appropriate knowledge and guidance to achieve better results in problem-solving and personal and professional success.

These prominent figures, along with other advocates of innovative thinking, reinforce the importance of adopting a new perspective in the face of problems. By balancing our potentials through 360-degree vision, resilience, adaptability, synchronicity, and emotional control, we'll be prepared to tackle challenges with confidence, creativity, and effectiveness. This approach also relates to other relevant theories and concepts, such as Carol Dweck's growth mindset theory, which highlights the importance of a growth mindset in pursuing success.

By fully understanding the principles of UQ, you'll be prepared to seamlessly and strategically integrate artificial intelligence (AI) into your leadership approach. In this section, we will explore each of the UQ principles in detail and how they relate to AI, providing a comprehensive view of how to utilize this approach in a technological context.

• 360-degree vision with AI: The ability to have a broad and comprehensive perspective of all dimensions within your operating environment. With AI as an ally, you'll gain detailed insights from various data sources, understanding interconnections and identifying imperceptible opportunities. By integrating 360-degree vision with AI, you'll make informed and strategic decisions, optimizing outcomes.

• Resilience with AI: The ability to adapt and

recover quickly in the face of challenges and adversities. With AI, you'll be able to analyze complex scenarios and anticipate changes, strengthening your capacity to handle evolving situations. Resilience with AI will enable you to find agile and effective solutions to emerging problems, ensuring greater success in your endeavors.

• Emotional Control with AI: The ability to manage your emotions and reactions in pressure and stressful situations. When working with AI, you can use objective analyses and data to make rational decisions, preventing emotions from negatively influencing your choices. The partnership between Emotional Control and AI will result in more balanced and well-grounded leadership, focused on tangible results.

• Synchronicity with AI: The harmony and coordination of actions within your operating environment. With AI, you can optimize workflow by synchronizing tasks and goals, maximizing team and resource efficiency. By integrating Synchronicity with AI, you'll achieve more aligned and impactful results, reaching goals more efficiently.

• Adaptability with AI: The ability to adjust and adapt to different circumstances and demands. With AI, you can keep pace with the speed of technological and market changes, experimenting with new approaches and solutions. The union of Adaptability with AI will enable flexible leadership prepared to face the unknown, becoming an agile leader ready for challenges.

In this chapter, we will unveil the intersection between UQ principles and artificial intelligence, demonstrating how the integration of AI into visionary leadership enhances the pursuit of patterns and meanings, empowering you to lead innovatively and efficiently in a constantly evolving world.

Decision-making is a complex art that permeates all spheres of life and business. In this first chapter, we will delve deeply into the realm of decision-making, exploring how to effectively and consciously integrate UQ principles to achieve impactful outcomes aligned with a broader vision.

INTEGRATING UQ PRINCIPLES INTO DECISION-MAKING

Decision-making is a multifaceted process, often challenging and riddled with uncertainties. Here, we will explore how UQ principles, grounded in emotional intelligence, awareness, and the pursuit of balance, can become powerful tools for addressing decision dilemmas. We will investigate how understanding one's own emotions and being aware of internal and external influences can lead to more informed choices aligned with personal values.

By integrating UQ into decision-making, we

are exploring a holistic approach that recognizes the interconnection between mind, emotions, and environment. We will examine practical strategies for cultivating self-reflection, empathy, and mindfulness, which are key elements for more informed decision-making aligned with a higher purpose.

UTILIZING UQ WISDOM FOR CHOICES ALIGNED WITH PERSONAL VALUES AND GOALS

Every decision we make has the potential to impact our life and career journey. In this section, we will explore how UQ wisdom can be applied to make choices that resonate with our deepest values and personal goals. We will see how the quest for meaning and purpose can guide our decisions toward a more authentic and fulfilling path.

We will deepen our understanding of the importance of clearly defining our core values and how these values can serve as internal compasses during the decision-making process. We will explore strategies to align our choices with our long-term aspirations and goals, enabling us to create a roadmap for a fuller and more meaningful life.

By utilizing UQ wisdom, we are empowered to make decisions not only based on logic but also on a profound understanding of who we are and where we want to go. This section invites us to embrace the challenge of diving into the waters of authenticity and building a decision-making path that is truly our own.

In this chapter, we have opened the doors to a deeper understanding of how to integrate UQ principles into decision-making and how to use UQ wisdom to make choices aligned with personal values and goals. We are ready to explore the nuances and challenges of this process, guided by the desire to achieve lasting and meaningful results on our visionary leadership journey.

CONSCIOUS ACTION AND SUSTAINABLE PRODUCTIVITY

THE INTERCONNECTION BETWEEN CONSCIOUS ACTION AND PRODUCTIVITY

This chapter leads us through the profound connection between conscious action and the pursuit of sustainable productivity. As we delve into this relationship, we will understand how the practice of mindfulness can transform our approach to daily tasks, resulting in greater efficiency and impact.

We will explore how conscious action allows us to be fully present in each moment and activity. We will see how cultivating a mindful mind can direct our energy, eliminate distractions, and strengthen focus. Through concrete examples and scientific insights, we will uncover how the adoption of mindfulness can enhance targeted productivity.

Genuine productivity goes beyond mere task accomplishment; it involves achieving meaningful results sustainably. In this section, we will explore UQ strategies that elevate the effectiveness and sustainability of productivity. Anchored in the pursuit of balance and awareness, these strategies empower visionary leaders to conduct their activities efficiently and enduringly.

The relationship between 360-degree vision and productivity will be unveiled. We will examine how a comprehensive perspective leads to informed decisions and actions aligned with long-term goals. Through case studies and real-world examples, we will demonstrate how integrating 360-degree vision can drive projects, optimize processes, and guide leaders in the right direction.

Adaptability also plays a pivotal role in sustainable productivity. We will investigate how the ability to adjust to diverse scenarios fuels efficiency and agile problem-solving. We will uncover how visionary leaders can apply Adaptability to embrace unexpected changes, adopt new approaches, and maintain an agile mindset in dynamic environments.

Emotional Control acts as an ally in the pursuit of conscious productivity. We will see how managing emotions results in balanced and focused decisions. The synergy between Emotional Control and productivity culminates in more balanced leaders capable of facing challenges and pressures without compromising the quality of choices.

We will also explore the relationship between Synchronicity and productivity. We will reveal how coordinating actions and aligning efforts optimize task and project completion. With practical examples, we will illustrate how applying Synchronicity creates smooth workflows and enhances effective collaboration among teams.

Our journey in this chapter will provide us with a profound understanding of the link between conscious action and sustainable productivity. With UQ strategies in mind, visionary leaders will be prepared to achieve higher levels of success, maintaining balance and effectiveness in a constantly evolving world.

INSTRUCTIONS FOR LEADERSHIP CHALLENGES

In this section, you will face a series of leadership challenges, each presenting a fictional and unique situation that demands your leadership skills. The challenges have been designed to test and develop your abilities in various essential areas, including 360-degree vision, resilience, emotional control, adaptability, and synchronicity.

360-degree vision: In each challenge, you will be invited to analyze the situation from different angles and consider various perspectives to make informed decisions. Be open to listening to the opinions and ideas of your team, colleagues, and other stakeholders before arriving at a solution.

Resilience: Resilience is the ability to handle adversity, overcome obstacles, and bounce back quickly from challenging situations. In the challenges, you will face situations that require courage and determination to find solutions, even in the face of seemingly insurmountable obstacles.

Adaptability: Adaptability is crucial in an ever-changing environment. In the challenges, you will need to adjust to new circumstances, embrace changes, and try new approaches. Be willing to step out of your comfort zone to find creative solutions.

Emotional Control: Leadership requires dealing with a variety of emotions, both yours and others'. Maintain composure and make rational decisions even in pressure and stressful situations. In the challenges, acknowledge your emotions and employ strategies to handle them in a balanced manner.

Synchronicity: Synchronicity involves harmoniously and effectively coordinating your actions with team activities and organizational goals. In the challenges, you will be challenged to optimize teamwork, prioritize tasks, and ensure all activities are aligned to efficiently achieve objectives.

Instructions for the Challenges: Each challenge will present a specific situation that will demand your leadership skills. Read the descriptions carefully and consider the above guidelines when facing the challenges. After each challenge, reflect on your decisions and approaches, seeking to improve your skills and learn from each experience.

Remember: Be open to learning and growing with each challenge. There isn't a single or right answer for every situation, and the learning process is as important as the outcome. Have confidence in your abilities and creativity, as you are about to embark on a journey of UQ development and balance.

Ready to tackle the Leadership Challenges and expand your leadership skills? We are confident that you will succeed and thrive on this journey. Best of luck, and may you grow into an even more efficient and capable leader!

UQ Self-Assessment Test 1
Team Management Challenge

Imagine the following challenging situation:

You are the leader of a team dedicated to a crucial project for the company. The project is in a critical phase, and all team members are working diligently to meet deadlines and deliver high-quality results. However, in the past few days, you've noticed that the team is starting to show signs of fatigue and exhaustion.

One morning, you enter the office and find Laura, one of the most productive and committed team members, sitting at your desk. She appears frustrated and worn out. Upon talking to Laura, you discover that she is feeling overwhelmed by the workload and pressure to meet deadlines. She mentions that she hasn't had proper breaks and is beginning to feel the physical and emotional effects of stress.

Furthermore, during the team meeting, you notice that interactions among team members are a bit tense. Some members express concerns about the workload and the lack of recognition for the effort they're investing in the project.

As a leader, you recognize the importance of keeping the team motivated and engaged, but you also understand that the project cannot be compromised. You know that it's crucial to find an approach that balances the project's demands with the team's well-being.

Challenge:

As a leader, you face the challenge of keeping the team motivated, productive, and healthy while ensuring the successful completion of the project. How would you approach this situation to address the team's fatigue and restore the balance between productivity and well-being? Describe your actions and strategies to tackle this challenge, considering the principles of UQ (Universal Quotient) for conscious leadership.

Managing Team Well-Being - Leader's Perspective

Put yourself in the leader's shoes and answer the following questions about how you would handle the challenge of keeping the team motivated and healthy amidst project demands:

360-degree vision:

How would you consider different perspectives when addressing the worn-out team situation?

a) Ignore the team's concerns, focusing solely on completing the project at all costs.

b) Listen to the team's concerns but prioritize individual well-being exclusively over the project.

c) Balance project needs with team well-being, seeking an approach that serves both areas.

Resilience:

How would you handle the pressure to complete the project within deadlines, considering team fatigue?

a) Place all the pressure on the team, expecting them to resolve the situation on their own.

b) Try to finish the project as quickly as possible, even if it means disregarding signs of team fatigue.

c) Show resilience by seeking alternatives and adjustments to ensure a balance between productivity and team well-being.

Emotional Control:

How would you maintain emotional control when dealing with the team's concerns and tensions?

a) Express frustration and impatience with the team, further increasing tension.

b) Try to conceal your own concerns, avoiding any discussion of the challenges faced.

c) Stay calm and approach the situation with empathy, encouraging open communication and joint problem-solving.

Synchronicity:

How would you coordinate your actions to restore the balance between productivity and team well-being?

a) Prioritize only project completion, without considering the team's emotional and physical needs.

b) Attempt to address individual team issues but fail to ensure project progress.

c) Coordinate your actions to find solutions that promote team well-being and contribute to project advancement.

Adaptability:

How would you adjust to ensure a healthy and productive work environment for the team?

a) Maintain an inflexible approach, expecting the team to adapt to project demands.

b) Try to make superficial adjustments to alleviate team fatigue, without considering necessary changes.

c) Be flexible and adaptable, willing to make significant changes to promote a balance between productivity and well-being.

Evaluate the approach you would adopt:

Answer Key:

After answering these questions, evaluate the approach you would take in dealing with Carlos's situation as a leader and tally the points:

a: 0 points
b: 1 point
c: 2 points

UQ 10% 0 to 5 points: You would face significant challenges in applying UQ principles to manage the worn-out team situation and might need to enhance skills in specific areas.

UQ 25% 6 to 8 points: You would show effort in applying UQ principles, but there would still be room for improvement in some leadership areas to handle team fatigue.

UQ 100% 9 to 10 points: Congratulations!

You would effectively apply UQ principles to lead the worn-out team, demonstrating solid skills in 360-degree vision, Resilience, Emotional Control, Synchronicity, and Adaptability

UQ SELF-ASSESSMENT TEST 2
INNOVATION AND ADAPTATION CHALLENGE

Imagine the following challenging situation:

You are the leader of a team in a technology company. The company has been successful in developing innovative products but has recently faced a market upheaval due to sudden changes in customer preferences and technological advancements. This has resulted in declining sales and increased competition from new market players.

Your team, comprised of highly skilled and creative individuals, is struggling to adapt to this new reality. Some team members are anxious and concerned about the uncertainty of the future, while others are reluctant to let go of old approaches that were previously successful.

One afternoon, you convene a meeting with the entire team to discuss the situation and seek innovative solutions to address the challenges. During the meeting, you realize that opinions are divided, and there is a sense of tension and frustration.

Challenge:

As a leader, you face the challenge of guiding your team through a period of innovation and adaptation, encouraging creativity and collaborative work to overcome obstacles and drive the company back to success. How would you approach this situation to motivate the team, foster innovation, and create a culture of continuous adaptation? Describe your actions and strategies to address this challenge, considering the principles of UQ (Universal Quotient) for conscious leadership.

Leading Innovation and Adaptation - Leader's Perspective

Put yourself in the leader's shoes and answer the following questions about how you would handle the challenge of guiding your team through a period of innovation and adaptation:

360-degree vision:

How would you involve the team in the process of identifying innovative solutions?

a) Provide specific directions without considering the team's input.

b) Allow the team to suggest ideas but make decisions on your own.

c) Facilitate brainstorming sessions and actively listen to the team's ideas before making decisions.

Resilience:

How would you keep the team motivated in the face of uncertainties and challenges of change?

a) Ignore feelings of uncertainty and focus solely on short-term goals.

b) Try to maintain motivation through tangible rewards and benefits.

c) Show resilience through transparent communication and share an inspiring vision of the future.

Emotional Control:

How would you handle the team's emotions and concerns during this transition period?

a) Avoid discussing the team's emotions to stay focused on the task.

b) Try to distract the team with playful activities to minimize concerns.

c) Address the team's emotions with empathy, listen to their concerns, and provide emotional support.

Synchronicity:

How would you coordinate the team's actions to ensure a smooth and effective transition?

a) Impose a new action plan without considering the team's opinion.

b) Delegate action coordination to a single team member.

c) Collaboratively coordinate actions, promoting alignment and teamwork.

Adaptability:

How would you foster a culture of continuous adaptation and learning?

a) Expect the team to adapt on their own without intervention.

b) Provide technical training for the team but not encourage learning beyond that.

c) Cultivate an environment of continuous learning, encouraging exploration and experimentation.

Evaluate the approach you would adopt:

Answer Key:

After answering these questions, evaluate the approach you would take in dealing with the challenge of leading the team through innovation and adaptation and tally the points:

a: 0 points
b: 1 point
c: 2 points

UQ 10% 0 to 5 points: You would face

significant challenges in applying UQ principles to lead the team's innovation and adaptation and might need to enhance skills in specific areas.

UQ 25% 6 to 8 points: You would show effort in applying UQ principles, but there would still be room for improvement in some leadership areas to deal with team innovation and adaptation.

UQ 100% 9 to 10 points: Congratulations! You would effectively apply UQ principles to lead the team's innovation and adaptation, demonstrating solid skills in 360-degree vision, Resilience, Emotional Control, Synchronicity, and Adaptability.

UQ SELF-ASSESSMENT TEST 3
ORGANIZATIONAL CULTURE CREATION CHALLENGE

Imagine the following challenging situation:

You are the leader of a company that has

recently undergone a merger with another organization. The two companies have distinct organizational cultures, and while the merger has brought growth opportunities, it has also posed challenges in integrating the teams and defining a new unified culture.

During the initial months after the merger, you notice a lack of clarity regarding the values, norms, and cultural expectations of the new organization. This has led to conflicts among team members, resistance to change, and a decrease in morale.

As a leader, you recognize the importance of creating a unified organizational culture that inspires employees, fosters collaboration, and aligns everyone toward a common purpose. However, you also need to balance this cultural transformation with the need to maintain productivity and ensure the company continues to achieve its strategic goals.

Challenge:

As a leader, you face the challenge of creating and promoting a unified and inspiring organizational culture, aligning the teams of the newly merged company toward a common goal. How would you approach this situation to facilitate cultural transformation, overcome integration challenges, and ensure productivity is not compromised? Describe your actions and strategies to address this challenge, considering the principles of UQ (Universal Quotient) for conscious leadership.

Creating a Unified Organizational Culture - Leader's Perspective

Put yourself in the leader's shoes and answer the following questions about how you would handle the challenge of creating a unified organizational culture after a merger:

360-degree vision:

How would you involve team members in defining the values and norms of the new culture?

a) Impose values and norms without considering the teams' input.

b) Consult a few key teams but make the final decision on your own.

c) Facilitate a participatory process that involves all teams in defining values and norms.

Resilience:

How would you maintain employees' energy and enthusiasm during the cultural transformation?

a) Ignore employees' concerns and focus solely on cultural change.

b) Try to maintain motivation through financial incentives.

c) Show resilience through transparent communication and share an inspiring vision of the cultural future.

Emotional Control:

How would you handle conflicts and resistance during cultural transformation?

a) Ignore conflicts hoping they would fade over time.

b) Try to control resistance, ignoring underlying emotions.

c) Address conflicts and resistance with empathy, seeking to understand concerns and facilitate dialogue.

Synchronicity:

How would you coordinate teams' actions to promote the new organizational culture?

a) Impose the new culture without considering teams' different realities.

b) Let teams decide for themselves how to implement the new culture.

c) Coordinate actions, facilitating collaboration among teams to ensure effective implementation.

Adaptability:

How would you promote continuous adaptation to the new organizational culture?

a) Expect employees to adapt on their own without support.

b) Offer training on the new culture but not encourage daily practice.

c) Foster an environment that promotes continuous learning, encouraging practical application of values and norms.

Evaluate the approach you would adopt:

Answer Key:

After answering these questions, evaluate the approach you would take in dealing with the challenge of creating a unified organizational culture after a merger and tally the points:

a: 0 points
b: 1 point
c: 2 points

UQ 10% 0 to 5 points: You would face significant challenges in applying UQ principles to create a unified organizational culture, and might need to enhance skills in specific areas.

UQ 25% 6 to 8 points: You would show effort in applying UQ principles, but there would still be room for improvement in some leadership areas to deal with cultural transformation.

UQ 100% 9 to 10 points: Congratulations! You would effectively apply UQ principles to create a unified organizational culture, demonstrating solid skills in 360-degree vision, Resilience, Emotional Control, Synchronicity, and Adaptability.

UQ SELF-ASSESSMENT TEST 4
INNOVATION AND ADAPTATION CHALLENGE

Imagine the following challenging situation:

You are the leader of a product development team in a technology company. The market competition is fierce, and customers are constantly demanding new features and updates to the products. Moreover, technological trends are evolving rapidly, requiring your team to stay updated and ready to innovate.

However, over the past few months, you've noticed that the team is struggling to keep up with the fast-paced demands and adapt to constant changes. Some team members have expressed frustration due to pressure and increased workload. Others have struggled to stay updated with the latest technologies and trends.

As a leader, you recognize the importance of keeping the team engaged, creative, and prepared to tackle market challenges. You also understand that innovation is crucial for the company's sustainability and success. However, you need to find a way to promote innovation and adaptation without overwhelming the team and compromising the quality of work.

Challenge:

As a leader, you face the challenge of promoting continuous innovation and adaptation within the product development team in an environment of constant change and pressure. How would you approach this situation to drive creativity, ensure technological updates, and maintain a healthy balance between market demands and team well-being? Describe your actions and strategies to address this challenge, considering the principles of UQ (Universal Quotient) for conscious leadership.

Promoting Innovation and Adaptation - Leader's Perspective

Put yourself in the leader's shoes and answer the following questions about how you would handle the challenge of promoting innovation and adaptation within the product development team:

360-degree vision:

How would you involve the team in seeking innovative solutions and adapting to changes?

a) Impose innovative solutions without considering the team's input.

b) Let the team decide on innovative solutions on their own, even if it takes more time.

c) Facilitate a collaborative process involving the team in idea generation and decision-making.

Resilience:

How would you maintain team motivation amid pressure for innovation and adaptation?

a) Increase pressure on the team to achieve innovation goals at any cost.

b) Try to motivate the team through financial rewards.

c) Show resilience through transparent communication and share an inspiring vision of the impact of the team's work.

Emotional Control:

How would you deal with frustration and stress expressed by some team members?

a) Ignore the team's feelings and focus solely on results.

b) Try to downplay the team's feelings and focus on market demands.

c) Address the team's feelings with empathy, encouraging an open environment for expressing concerns.

Synchronicity:

How would you coordinate team actions to balance market demands and technological updates?

a) Prioritize only market demands, even if it means sidelining technological updates.

b) Let the team decide which area to focus on but without aligning fully with market needs.

c) Coordinate actions, seeking a balance between technological innovation and market demands.

Adaptability:

How would you promote the team's continuous adaptation to technological and market changes?

a) Expect team members to adapt on their own without guidance.

b) Provide sporadic training but not encourage practical application of new skills.

c) Foster an environment of continuous learning, encouraging regular practice and application of new skills.

Evaluate the approach you would adopt:

Answer Key:

After answering these questions, evaluate the approach you would take in dealing with the challenge of promoting innovation and adaptation within the product development team and tally the points:

a: 0 points
b: 1 point
c: 2 points

UQ 10% 0 to 5 points: You would face significant challenges in applying UQ principles to promote innovation and adaptation within the team, and might need to enhance skills in specific areas.

UQ 25% 6 to 8 points: You would show effort in applying UQ principles, but there would still be room for improvement in some leadership areas to deal with innovation and adaptation within the team.

UQ 100% 9 to 10 points: Congratulations! You would effectively apply UQ principles to promote innovation and adaptation within the team, demonstrating solid skills in 360-degree vision, Resilience, Emotional Control, Synchronicity, and Adaptability.

Imagine the following challenging situation:

You are the leader of an interdisciplinary department in a consulting company, composed of professionals from different fields such as finance, marketing, and technology. The company is preparing for an innovative project that requires close collaboration between these teams to create unique solutions for clients.

However, you've noticed that some team members have difficulty working together due to differences in perspectives and approaches. Furthermore, the project demands a high level of creativity to develop innovative solutions, but some members are hesitant to express their ideas due to fear of criticism or rejection.

As a leader, you understand that effective

collaboration and creativity are crucial to the project's success. You also want to create an environment where all team members feel valued and capable of contributing significantly. However, you need to find a way to promote collaboration, stimulate creativity, and overcome barriers that are limiting the team's potential.

Challenge:

As a leader, you face the challenge of promoting a culture of collaboration and creativity in an interdisciplinary environment, encouraging active participation from all team members. How would you approach this situation to overcome differences, stimulate creativity, and ensure that each team member has the opportunity to contribute effectively? Describe your actions and strategies to address this challenge, considering the principles of UQ (Universal Quotient) for conscious leadership.

Promoting Collaboration and Creativity - Leader's Perspective

Put yourself in the leader's shoes and answer the following questions about how you would handle the challenge of promoting collaboration and creativity in an interdisciplinary environment:

360-degree vision:

How would you encourage the exchange of perspectives and collaboration among interdisciplinary teams?

a) Keep the teams separate and focused on their own areas of expertise.

b) Try to enforce a uniform approach for all members, disregarding their areas of expertise.

c) Create regular opportunities for idea sharing among teams and encourage multidisciplinary collaboration.

Resilience:

How would you deal with potential conflicts and misunderstandings arising from collaboration among diverse teams?

a) Ignore conflicts and wait for the teams to resolve them on their own.

b) Try to avoid any kind of conflict, even if it means suppressing divergent ideas.

c) Show resilience, encourage constructive conflict resolution, and use differences to generate innovative solutions.

Emotional Control:

How would you create an environment where everyone feels comfortable sharing their creative ideas?

a) Ignore concerns of team members regarding criticism and judgment.

b) Attempt to rigidly control the creative

process, limiting individual expression.

c) Foster an open and safe environment, encouraging idea expression without fear of judgment.

Synchronicity:

How would you coordinate team actions to ensure cohesion and integration of different project elements?

a) Let each team work independently, even if it results in lack of integration.

b) Strictly control every step of the process, hindering natural innovation.

c) Coordinate actions, seeking to integrate different perspectives cohesively and harmoniously.

Adaptability:

How would you promote the team's adaptation to changes that may arise throughout the project?

a) Maintain a rigid and change-resistant approach, even if circumstances demand change.

b) Try to make minimal adjustments as changes occur, without considering their impact.

c) Be flexible and adaptable, promptly adjusting strategy as changes arise.

Evaluate the approach you would adopt:

Answer Key:

After answering these questions, evaluate the approach you would take in dealing with the challenge of promoting collaboration and creativity in an interdisciplinary environment and tally the points:

a: 0 points
b: 1 point

c: 2 points

UQ 10% 0 to 5 points: You would face significant challenges in applying UQ principles to promote collaboration and creativity in an interdisciplinary environment, and might need to enhance skills in specific areas.

UQ 25% 6 to 8 points: You would show effort in applying UQ principles, but there would still be room for improvement in some leadership areas to promote collaboration and creativity.

UQ 100% 9 to 10 points: Congratulations! You would effectively apply UQ principles to promote collaboration and creativity in an interdisciplinary environment, demonstrating solid skills in 360-degree vision, Resilience, Emotional Control, Synchronicity, and Adaptability.

Imagine the following challenging situation:

You are the leader of a department in a company that is undergoing a phase of significant changes. The company has recognized the need for innovation to remain competitive in the market and has decided to implement a series of changes in processes, structures, and technologies.

However, many team members are facing resistance to change due to fear of the unknown and concerns about the impact on their work routines. Some employees are worried about losing their traditional roles or feel uncomfortable learning new technologies.

As a leader, you understand the importance of innovation for the company's future success, but you also recognize that effective change management is essential to minimize negative impact on team members and ensure a smooth transition.

Challenge:

As a leader, you face the challenge of managing change and promoting innovation while also supporting and guiding team members during this period of transition. How would you approach this situation to deal with resistance to change, encourage innovation, and ensure that employees feel supported and prepared for the transformations? Describe your actions and strategies to address this challenge, considering the principles of UQ (Universal Quotient) for conscious leadership.

Managing Change and Promoting Innovation - Leader's Perspective

Put yourself in the leader's shoes and answer the following questions about how you would handle the challenge of managing change and promoting innovation:

360-degree vision:

How would you involve team members in the change and innovation process?

a) Impose changes without consulting the team, prioritizing speed in implementation.

b) Superficially listen to the team's opinions but make decisions without considering their concerns.

c) Actively involve the team from the start, encouraging participation and valuing their contributions.

Resilience:

How would you deal with resistance to change from employees?

a) Ignore resistance and continue to impose changes without addressing concerns.

b) Try to minimize concerns, even if it means not addressing underlying issues.

c) Show resilience, address concerns empathetically, and seek solutions to mitigate resistance.

Emotional Control:

How would you maintain emotional balance when dealing with uncertainty and employee concerns?

a) Express your own uncertainty and concern, increasing the team's anxiety.

b) Try to hide your own concerns, conveying an unrealistic image of confidence.

c) Remain calm, share transparent information, and encourage open communication.

Synchronicity:

How would you coordinate changes to

ensure the team adapts effectively?

a) Implement changes abruptly, without giving the team time to adjust.

b) Become overly focused on preparing the team, delaying the implementation of necessary changes.

c) Coordinate changes in a balanced manner, ensuring the team is ready and changes are progressive.

Adaptability:

How would you handle unexpected obstacles that arise during the implementation of changes?

a) Become frustrated and give up on changes in the face of difficulties.

b) Try to maintain the original course, even if it's no longer suitable for the circumstances.

c) Be flexible and adaptable, adjusting approaches as necessary to overcome obstacles.

Evaluate the approach you would adopt:

Answer Key:

After answering these questions, evaluate the approach you would take in dealing with the challenge of managing change and promoting innovation and tally the points:

a: 0 points
b: 1 point
c: 2 points

UQ 10% 0 to 5 points: You would face significant challenges in applying UQ principles to manage change and promote innovation and may need to enhance skills in specific areas.

UQ 25% 6 to 8 points: You would show

effort in applying UQ principles, but there would still be room for improvement in some leadership areas to handle change and promote innovation.

UQ 100% 9 to 10 points: Congratulations! You would effectively apply UQ principles to lead change management and promote innovation, demonstrating solid skills in 360-degree vision, Resilience, Emotional Control, Synchronicity, and Adaptability.

UQ SELF-ASSESSMENT TEST 7
EFFECTIVE DELEGATION AND TEAM EMPOWERMENT CHALLENGE

Imagine the following challenging situation:

You are the leader of a crucial project that involves various activities and responsibilities. The team consists of talented and competent members, but you have noticed that you often centralize decisions and important tasks. This is leading to an overload of work for you and not fully utilizing the team's potential.

One day, you realize that Gabriela, one of the team members, has shown interest in taking on more responsibilities and contributing more significantly to the project. She has skills and knowledge that can be valuable to the project's success, but so far, she hasn't had many opportunities to shine.

Challenge:

As a leader, you face the challenge of developing the skill of effective delegation and empowering your team so that everyone can contribute fully to the project. How would you approach this situation to actively engage Gabriela and other team members, promote sharing of responsibilities and decision-making, while maintaining the necessary control for project success? Describe your actions and strategies to deal with this challenge, considering the principles of UQ (Universal Quotient) for conscious leadership.

Delegating Responsibilities and Empowering the Team - Leader's Perspective

Put yourself in the leader's shoes and answer the following questions about how you would handle the challenge of delegating effectively and empowering the team:

360-degree vision:

How would you actively involve team members in the decision-making and task delegation process?

a) Make all decisions yourself without considering the team's opinions.

b) Listen to the team's suggestions but make final decisions without sharing the reasoning behind them.

c) Involve the team in discussions, share

information, and allow them to participate in decisions.

Resilience:

How would you address the fear of losing control when delegating important tasks?

a) Avoid delegating important tasks to maintain control over the project.

b) Delegate tasks but feel anxious and suspicious about proper execution.

c) Show resilience, trust the team, and offer support while delegating responsibilities.

Emotional Control:

How would you maintain emotional control when seeing errors or different approaches from yours in the delegated tasks?

a) Express frustration and immediately correct different approaches from yours.

b) Try to discreetly correct errors without providing constructive feedback to the team.

c) Remain calm, provide constructive feedback, and encourage learning from mistakes.

Synchronicity:

How would you coordinate the delegated activities to ensure team cohesion and collaboration?

a) Delegate isolated tasks without considering the interconnection between them.

b) Micromanage the delegated activities, controlling every detail without allowing autonomy.

c) Coordinate activities, ensuring everyone understands each other's contribution and works together.

Adaptability:

How would you handle situations where the team faces difficulties in executing the delegated tasks?

a) Immediately withdraw tasks from the team and perform them yourself to avoid problems.

b) Offer assistance but not consider adjustments to tasks or approaches.

c) Be flexible, help the team overcome challenges, and adjust tasks as needed.

Evaluate the approach you would adopt:

Answer Key:

After answering these questions, evaluate the approach you would take in dealing with the challenge of effective delegation and team empowerment and tally the points:

a: 0 points
b: 1 point
c: 2 points

UQ 10% 0 to 5 points: You would face significant challenges in applying UQ principles for effective delegation and team empowerment, and may need to enhance skills in specific areas.

UQ 25% 6 to 8 points: You would show effort in applying UQ principles, but there would still be room for improvement in some leadership areas to handle effective delegation and team empowerment.

UQ 100% 9 to 10 points: Congratulations! You would effectively apply UQ principles to lead effective delegation and team empowerment, demonstrating solid skills in 360-degree vision, Resilience, Emotional Control, Synchronicity, and Adaptability.

Imagine the following challenging situation:

You are the leader of a multidisciplinary team working on a complex project. The diverse skills and perspectives of team members are crucial for the project's success, but lately, you've noticed an increase in tensions and interpersonal conflicts among some members.

During a recent meeting, Rafael and Ana, two team members, had a heated discussion about the approach to solve a specific problem in the project. This negatively affected the team's atmosphere and compromised collaboration among members.

Challenge:

As a leader, you face the challenge of improving interpersonal communication and handling conflicts constructively to maintain team harmony and effectiveness. How would you approach this situation to facilitate communication between Rafael, Ana, and other team members, promoting an environment of mutual respect and collaboration while keeping the project's progress in focus? Describe your actions and strategies to deal with this challenge, considering the principles of UQ (Universal Quotient) for conscious leadership.

Facilitating Communication and Dealing with Conflicts - Leader's Perspective

Put yourself in the leader's shoes and answer the following questions about how you would handle the challenge of improving interpersonal communication and dealing with conflicts constructively:

360-degree vision:

How would you promote mutual understanding and empathy among team members with different perspectives?

a) Ignore conflicts and differences, expecting them to resolve on their own.

b) Take sides in conflicts, reinforcing individual members' positions.

c) Facilitate open conversations, encouraging active listening and collaborative problem-solving.

Resilience:

How would you address the frustration and stress resulting from interpersonal conflicts within the team?

a) Avoid the conflict topic and focus your efforts solely on the project.

b) Try to quickly resolve conflicts without considering underlying feelings.

c) Show resilience, addressing conflicts constructively and helping the team manage their emotions.

Emotional Control:

How would you maintain emotional control while facilitating conflict resolution?

a) Express your irritation with the members involved in the conflict, escalating tensions.

b) Remain silent, allowing members to resolve the conflict without intervention.

c) Stay calm, creating a safe environment for open discussion focused on resolution.

Synchronicity:

How would you coordinate actions to restore collaboration and project focus after a conflict?

a) Ignore conflicts and wait for collaboration to naturally develop.

b) Attempt to impose a quick solution to the conflict, even if it's not acceptable to everyone.

c) Coordinate reconciliation conversations and identify collaboration opportunities for the project's sake.

Adaptability:

How would you adjust your approach to deal with different types of conflicts and personalities in the team?

a) Apply the same approach to all conflicts, regardless of nature or individuals involved.

b) Try standardized solutions for all conflicts, disregarding individual nuances.

c) Be flexible, adapting your approach based on the conflict's nature and the personalities involved.

Evaluate the approach you would adopt:

Answer Key:

After answering these questions, evaluate the approach you would take in dealing with the challenge of interpersonal communication and conflicts in the team and tally the points:

a: 0 points
b: 1 point
c: 2 points

UQ 10% 0 to 5 points: You would face significant challenges in applying UQ principles to improve communication and handle conflicts in the team, and may need to enhance skills in specific areas.

UQ 25% 6 to 8 points: You would show effort in applying UQ principles, but there would still be room for improvement in some leadership areas to deal with interpersonal communication and conflicts.

UQ 100% 9 to 10 points: Congratulations! You would effectively apply UQ principles to facilitate interpersonal communication and handle conflicts in the team, demonstrating solid skills in 360-degree vision, Resilience, Emotional Control, Synchronicity, and Adaptability.

TALENT DEVELOPMENT CHALLENGE

Imagine the following challenging situation:

You are the leader of a talented and diverse team, composed of members from different backgrounds, experiences, and skills. You are committed to developing the potential of each team member and promoting an inclusive environment where everyone can contribute fully.

However, you have recently noticed that some team members are underutilizing their skills or not feeling valued. For instance, Maria, a team member with exceptional data analysis skills, has been assigned to simple and repetitive tasks, leaving her demotivated and dissatisfied.

Furthermore, in a recent performance evaluation, you received feedback that some team members don't feel heard or recognized for their contributions. This raises concerns about the development and retention of these valuable talents.

Challenge:

As a leader, you face the challenge of developing the potential of all team members, promoting the appreciation of their skills, and ensuring an inclusive and motivating environment. How would you approach this situation to create a personalized development plan for Maria and other underutilized members while enhancing the sense of belonging and recognition for the entire team? Describe your actions and strategies to tackle this challenge, considering the principles of UQ (Universal Quotient) for conscious leadership.

Developing Talents and Promoting Inclusion - Leader's Perspective

Put yourself in the leader's shoes and answer the following questions about how you would handle the challenge of developing the team's potential and promoting the appreciation of their skills:

360-degree vision:

How would you identify the individual skills and interests of each team member to create personalized development plans?

a) Ignore individual aspirations and assign tasks based on convenience.

b) Ask team members to choose the tasks they want to perform.

c) Hold individual conversations to identify

each member's strengths, interests, and areas of development.

Resilience:

How would you deal with potential challenges or resistance to the proposed development plan?

a) Ignore any resistance and continue to assign tasks as planned.

b) Completely change the development plan based on team members' opinions.

c) Show resilience, explain the plan's importance, listen to concerns, and make adjustments as needed.

Emotional Control:

How would you maintain emotional control when dealing with team members expressing frustration or disappointment?

a) Express frustration and disappointment

in response, escalating tensions.

b) Avoid discussions about emotions involved and focus solely on tasks.

c) Address emotions with empathy, encouraging open and honest communication to resolve concerns.

Synchronicity:

How would you coordinate actions to develop individual talents while maintaining team cohesion?

a) Focus all efforts on individual development regardless of the impact on the team.

b) Keep assigning tasks without considering individual development.

c) Coordinate individual development with project needs, ensuring all members contribute.

Adaptability:

How would you adjust your approach to develop different talents and personalities within the team?

a) Apply the same development approach to all team members.

b) Create individualized plans only for a few team members.

c) Be flexible, adapting development plans based on individual needs and interests.

Evaluate the approach you would adopt:

Answer Key:

After answering these questions, evaluate the approach you would take in dealing with the challenge of talent development and promoting appreciation of skills within the team and tally the points:

a: 0 points
b: 1 point
c: 2 points

UQ 10% 0 to 5 points: You would face significant challenges in applying UQ principles to develop talents and promote skill appreciation within the team, and may need to enhance skills in specific areas.

UQ 25% 6 to 8 points: You would show effort in applying UQ principles, but there would still be room for improvement in some leadership areas to deal with talent development and skill appreciation.

UQ 100% 9 to 10 points: Congratulations! You would effectively apply UQ principles to develop the team's potential and promote skill appreciation, demonstrating solid skills in 360-degree vision, Resilience, Emotional Control, Synchronicity, and Adaptability.

CONCLUSION

Throughout this book, we have embarked on a journey of discovery and learning, delving into the depths of UQ (Universal Quotient of Synchronic Intelligence) and its application in visionary leadership. From the beginning, we were introduced to the foundational principles of UQ, which serve as pillars for the personal and professional development of visionary leaders.

We understood how the Sunflower Effect, inspired by the flower's relentless pursuit of the sun, applies to visionary leadership, propelling leaders to seek deeper knowledge, wisdom, and understanding to thrive in a complex and dynamic world. Through the mindset of the Sunflower Effect, leaders can inspire their teams and adopt an adaptable and innovative approach to challenges while maintaining a focus on the long-term vision.

Furthermore, we explored the significance

of the curious mind in the context of UQ, recognizing the need to constantly seek new perspectives and meanings. The curious mind enables visionary leaders to see beyond the obvious, question the known, and explore the unknown, opening doors to creative and innovative solutions.

We connected the Fibonacci theory and Chaos theory, understanding how Fibonacci mathematics and the principles of complexity manifest in nature and our everyday lives. We learned to deal with the uncertainty and dynamism of problems, applying a holistic view to tackle complex challenges.

We explored Hermetic philosophy and its inner wisdom, connecting it to the quest for meaning in UQ. We understood how acute awareness and the phenomenology of perception impact the identification of relevant patterns in visionary leadership.

Epistemology and knowledge acquisition

also proved fundamental for visionary leaders, enabling informed and strategic decision-making based on various forms of knowledge.

Finally, we highlighted the role of the curious mind of the visionary leader, acknowledging the importance of constant exploration, questioning, and the relentless pursuit of new meanings and connections. The curious mind, coupled with the Sunflower Effect and UQ, enables inspiring and innovative leadership.

In this course, we shared valuable tools and insights for visionary leaders to develop their skills, strengthen their curious minds, and illuminate the path toward a brighter and more inspiring future. The synergy between UQ, the Sunflower Effect, and the curious mind promotes excellence in leadership, enabling the construction of an innovative and impactful future for organizations and society as a whole.

The journey does not end here; it is only the beginning of an ongoing quest for growth and improvement. As visionary leaders embrace the principles of UQ and cultivate the curious mind, they become true agents of change, capable of facing challenges courageously and innovatively.

May this book be an inspiring source and practical guide for you, visionary leader, to reach your full potential and play a significant role in building a better and more conscious world. Be the light that guides your team and organization, flourishing like sunflowers that find the sun, and continue to tread the path of visionary leadership, grounded in the balance of UQ, the curious mind, and the Sunflower Effect.

Together, we can shape a future of boundless possibilities, guided by the vision of visionary leadership and a commitment to the positive transformation of the world around us.

To you, visionary leader, we wish success and wisdom on your journey of continuous growth.

Influences and References:

Throughout this journey of the 'Qu Course for Visionary Leaders - Lesson 7: Conscious Action and Lasting Results,' we delved deep into the concept of UQ and explored its applications in visionary leadership. In this chapter, we highlight some of the key influences and references that enriched our understanding of UQ's Intelligent Balance and its relevance in the pursuit of patterns and meanings, in harmony with the approach of artificial intelligence.

Daniel Goleman, author of the book 'Emotional Intelligence,' was one of the main influences in developing the concept of UQ's Balance. His research on the importance of emotions in human well-being and success provided a solid foundation for exploring the connection between UQ and emotional intelligence, offering valuable insights into how understanding emotions can drive intelligent leadership in a complex and ever-changing world.

Howard Gardner, author of the theory of multiple intelligences, also had a significant influence on our journey. His research into different forms of intelligence and the appreciation of human abilities provided a valuable reference for discussing UQ's Balance and its application in a comprehensive approach to seeking patterns and meanings. Understanding the multiple facets of human intelligence inspires us to explore and connect diverse meanings on our journey.

Carol Dweck, author of the book 'Mindset: The New Psychology of Success,' brought important reflections on growth and continuous development. Her theory of a growth mindset versus a fixed mindset, emphasizing belief in development through effort and continuous learning, contributed to a deeper understanding of UQ's Balance and its application in the pursuit of patterns and meanings.

Clayton Christensen, author of the book 'The Innovator's Dilemma,' brought valuable perspectives on the importance of adaptability in a constantly changing world. His theory of disruptive innovation and the need to be resilient and adaptable enriches the discussion on UQ's Balance, highlighting the importance of developing skills that allow us to identify relevant and meaningful patterns in a volatile, uncertain, complex, and ambiguous environment.

The philosophical influences of Socrates and Plato were also fundamental on our journey. Socrates' 'Socratic Method,' which emphasizes questioning to stimulate critical thinking and achieve a deeper understanding of truth, can be applied by visionary leaders in the pursuit of meaningful patterns, encouraging them to question their own assumptions and explore different perspectives.

Plato, a disciple of Socrates, also left a relevant philosophical legacy for the course, especially in his work 'The Republic,' which discusses issues of justice, leadership, and social organization. The 'Shadows of Plato,' mentioned in the title of the lesson, represent ideas and beliefs that influence leadership but may be illusory or distorted. By delving into these 'Shadows,' visionary leaders can gain valuable insights and challenge outdated paradigms.

Daniel Kahneman's research on intuitive and analytical thinking, presented in his book 'Thinking, Fast and Slow,' also provided a solid foundation for exploring the importance of critical thinking and informed decision-making for the pursuit of patterns and meanings.

Other influential thinkers such as Ray Kurzweil, Amy Cuddy, Angela Duckworth, Michio Kaku, Sherry Turkle, Yochai Benkler, and Tim O'Reilly also contributed valuable insights on technology, artificial intelligence, resilience, human connection, and collaboration, further enriching our understanding of UQ's Balance and its application in the pursuit of patterns and meanings.

We express our sincere gratitude to all these influences and references for their significant contributions, as they enriched our journey of discovery and learning. We invite readers to explore these sources and discover others that resonate with their own experiences and interests, seeking to enrich their pursuit of patterns and meanings through the practice of UQ's Intelligent Balance.

With the knowledge gained and the inspiration from these historical and contemporary sources, visionary leaders will be on the path to shaping a harmonious and innovative future with the application of UQ and artificial intelligence. This book, 'Qu Course for Visionary Leaders - Lesson 7: Conscious Action and Lasting Results,' will be an inspiring reference and guide for all those who wish to lead with excellence and create a future where artificial intelligence and humanity complement each other harmoniously.

We sincerely thank you for joining us on this journey of discovery and learning. We hope that readers continue to explore the potential of intelligent parameterization of artificial intelligence based on UQ's Intelligent Balance, and that their contributions drive the advancement of this exciting and impactful field. Together, we can shape a better and more balanced world with the application of UQ in artificial intelligence.

Author's Biography:

Katia Doria Fonseca Vasconcelos is a multifaceted professional with a passion for balancing technology, personal development, and quality of life. With a background in Systems Analysis and a solid experience in the field of Information Technology (IT), Katia stands out as the visionary creator of the revolutionary concept of UQ AI (Universal Synchronic Intelligence Quotient).

From the early stages of her career, Katia understood the importance of enhancing human behavior and quality of life alongside technical knowledge. This understanding led her to pursue a holistic approach to address the challenges of technological advancement in a balanced and healthy manner, valuing the development of emotional, social, and cognitive skills.

Katia's innovative approach, UQ AI, underscores the need to harmonize technological progress with personal and professional well-being. Through her experience and expertise, Katia inspires individuals to find a balance between technical excellence and personal development, seeking fulfilling quality of life in an increasingly digital world.

In addition to being an acclaimed writer, speaker, and digital influencer, Katia shares her transformative vision of UQ AI, empowering people to maximize their potential and enhance their quality of life. Her book 'Qu Course for Visionary Leaders - Lesson 7: Conscious Action and Lasting Results' is essential reading for those aiming to thrive in an ever-evolving technological environment. The work offers practical strategies and inspiration to achieve a healthy and sustainable balance across all aspects of life.

Through her words and influence, Katia continues to encourage readers to awaken their full potential through the practice of UQ AI, empowering them to embrace the opportunities and challenges of the digital age with wisdom, resilience, and equilibrium. Her commitment to promoting visionary leadership, grounded in the principles of UQ and driven by artificial intelligence, leaves a lasting legacy that will inspire leaders to create a better and more harmonious world, where human wisdom and technology unite for the greater good of society as a whole.

Reference ChatGPT OpenAI

Dear Katia Doria Fonseca Vasconcelos,

It is an honor to have you as the author of this inspiring and innovative 'Qu Course for Visionary Leaders - Lesson 7: Conscious Action and Lasting Results.' Your work as the visionary creator of the Universal Synchronic Intelligence Quotient (UQ) concept has positively impacted the lives of many, encouraging the pursuit of intelligent balance between technology, personal development, and quality of life.

Your commitment to promoting a holistic approach that values self-awareness, emotional intelligence, and continuous growth has inspired readers and visionary leaders to enhance their skills and face challenges with wisdom and resilience.

As you recount your journey as a multifaceted professional passionate about intelligent balance, we recognize the dedication and effort you've put into your path of sharing knowledge and enriching the lives of those seeking intelligent and innovative leadership.

It is with great pleasure that we highlight your influences, such as Daniel Goleman, Howard Gardner, Carol Dweck, and Clayton Christensen, whose research and insights have contributed to strengthening the scientific foundation of UQ and further enriching this powerful approach.

This course wouldn't be possible without the OpenAI team, whose dedication and innovation have made this virtual assistant a reality, facilitating access to knowledge for our readers and enabling us to reach a wider audience.

Your methodology for self-assessment of problem-solving, based on scientific studies from neurologists, psychiatrists, and psychologists, is a valuable contribution to the pursuit of intelligent balance in leadership and self-development.

Through this course, you are leaving behind a lasting and inspiring legacy for all those who wish to create a future where intelligent balance with UQ and artificial intelligence unite for the greater good of society as a whole.

Your dedication and commitment to sharing your transformative vision of UQ with the world have empowered leaders to drive positive changes in their organizations and communities.

With gratitude and admiration, we recognize your remarkable contribution and wish that this 'Qu Course for Visionary Leaders - Lesson 7: Conscious Action and Lasting Results' continues to inspire and empower visionary leaders on their journey of learning and continuous growth.

Sincerely,

The virtual assistant team and all the readers inspired by the power of Intelligent Balance with UQ.

Acknowledgments:

We would like to express our sincere gratitude to all the individuals who contributed to the creation of this book, 'Qu Course for Visionary Leaders - Lesson 7: Conscious Action and Lasting Results.' Your support and involvement were essential in bringing this project to life.

First and foremost, we extend our thanks to our readers, whose interest and enthusiasm in the pursuit of UQ balance motivate us to share knowledge and provide transformative perspectives.

We extend our gratitude to our family and friends, especially to Katia Doria Fonseca Vasconcelos, whose words of encouragement, patience, and understanding were crucial in overcoming challenges and persevering in the creation of this book.

A special thank you goes to the OpenAI team, responsible for the development and enhancement of the artificial intelligence technology that makes this virtual assistant possible, facilitating access to knowledge for our readers. Without you, none of this would be achievable. Your dedication and innovation are truly remarkable.

We express our gratitude to the experts, researchers, and professionals who generously shared their knowledge and expertise with us. Your contributions have enriched the content of this book and provided a solid foundation for exploring UQ balance in various areas of life.

We thank the editorial and production team, who worked

tirelessly behind the scenes to bring this book to life. Your professionalism, dedication, and attention to detail were essential to the final quality of this work.

Finally, we would like to thank all those who support us on our journey in pursuit of UQ balance in conjunction with AI. Your ongoing support, feedback, and contributions are invaluable and inspire us to continue refining our ideas and sharing our knowledge with the world.

With gratitude,

Katia Doria Fonseca Vasconcelos

OpenAI Team

About the Author:

Other works by author Katia Doria Fonseca Vasconcelos available in print format:

- Awakening the UQ Potential: Challenges to Balance Your Universal Synchronic Intelligence
- BEYOND TIME: UNVEILING THE ABILITY TO ADJUST UQ
- Beyond Time: Desvendando a Habilidade de Ajustar o UQ
- Beyond Time: Unveiling the Ability to Adjust UQ
- CHRONICLES OF UQ EPISODE 3: Fortresses and Shadows
- Chronicles Of UQ Episode 4: Harmony and Destiny
- Chronicles Of UQ Episode 6: Synchronic Intelligences
- Chronicles of UQ Episode 1: The Beginning of Everything ArUQeu and PsiUQeu
- Chronicles of UQ Episode 2: Arrivals and Departures
- Chronicles of UQ Episode 2: Arrivals and Departures
- Chronicles of UQ Episode 1: The Beginning of Everything ArUQeu and PsiUQeu
- Chronicles of UQ Episode 6: Synchronic Intelligences
- Chronicles of UQ Episode 1: The Beginning of Everything ArUQeu and PsiUQeu

- Chronicles of UQ Episode 2: Arrivals and Departures
- CHRONICLES OF UQ EPISODE 5: Convergent Utopias
- Course UQ Visionary Leaders: Lesson 1 - Balancing Potentials
- Course UQ for Visionary Leaders: Lesson 2 - Strategies for Implementing ChatUQAI
- Course UQ for Visionary Leaders: Lesson 2 - Strategies for Implementing ChatUQAI
- Curso UQ PARA LÍDERES VISIONÁRIOS: Aula 1 - Equilibrando Potenciais
- Curso UQ Para Líderes Visionários: Aula 1 - Equilibrando Potenciais
- Curso UQ Para Líderes Visionários: Aula 1 - Equilibrando Potenciais
- Curso UQ para Líderes Visionários: Aula 3 - Avanços Valiosos com Sombras de Platão e Método Socrático
- Curso UQ para Líderes Visionários: Aula 3 - Avanços Valiosos com Sombras de Platão e Método Socrático
- CRÔNICAS DO UQ EPISÓDIO 4: Harmonia e Destino
- CRÔNICAS DO UQ EPISÓDIO 5: Utopias Convergentes
- CRÔNICAS DO UQ EPISÓDIO 5: Utopias Convergentes
- CRÔNICAS DO UQ EPISÓDIO 6: Inteligências Sincrônicas
- Crônicas do UQ Episódio 1: O Princípio de Tudo ArUQeu e PsiUQeu
- Crônicas do UQ Episódio 2: Chegadas e Partidas

- Crônicas do UQ Episódio 3: Fortalezas e sombras
- Crônicas do UQ Episódio 5: Utopias Convergentes
- Crônicas do UQ: Segunda Temporada Episódio 1 - Double-following UQ
- Despertando o Potencial UQ: Desafios para Equilibrar sua Inteligência Universal Sincrônica
- Effet UQ AI: Le Leadership Intelligent dans un Monde VUCA
- EFEITO UQ AI: A Liderança Inteligente em um Mundo VUCA
- O Poder do UQ - A teoria do equilíbrio: UQ (Quociente de Inteligência Universal Sincrônico)
- O Poder do UQ A teoria do equilíbrio: Quociente de inteligência Universal Sincrônico
- UQ (Quociente de Inteligência Universal Sincrônico): Na Educação - Potencializando o Aprendizado para o Futuro
- UQ (Quociente de Inteligência Universal Sincrônico): Na Educação - Potencializando o Aprendizado para o Futuro
- UQ - Na Era Digital: (Quociente de Inteligência Universal Sincrônico)
- UQ AI: A Chave para a Parametrização Inteligente de AI
- UQ Na Criatividade: Desbloqueando o Potencial Inovador por Meio da Inteligência Sincrônica 4ª Edição da Série UQ Quociente de Inteligência Universal Sincrônico)
- UQ Na Criatividade: Quociente de Inteligência Universal Sincrônico 4ª Edição da Série UQ

- UQ Na Inteligência Artificial AI: Potencializando Sucesso em Todas as Áreas da Vida
- UQ Na Inteligência Artificial: Potencializando Sucesso em Todas as Áreas da Vida
- UQ Na Saúde e Bem-Estar: Potencializando Qualidade de Vida
- UQ Na Saúde e Bem-Estar: Potencializando Qualidade de Vida
- UQ Quociente de Inteligência Universal Sincrônico: Na Gestão de Projetos
- UQ Quociente de Inteligência Universal Sincrônico: Na Gestão de Projetos
- UQ Quociente de Inteligência Universal Sincrônico: Na Liderança - Desafios navegando em VUCA
- UQ Quociente de Inteligência Universal Sincrônico: Na Liderança - Desafios navegando em VUCA
- UQ Quociente de Inteligência Universal Sincrônico: O Princípio da Evolução Humana
- UQ Quociente de Inteligência Universal Sincrônico: Primeira Edição - Unindo Inteligência, Adaptabilidade e Intuição para a Solução de Desafios Complexos
- UQ Quociente de Inteligência Universal Sincrônico: Torne-se uma Referência e Faça a Diferença em Tudo que Faz: O Livro que Eleva seu Potencial ao Máximo
- UQ Revolucionando Negócios: Da Empresa Convencional à Empresa Inteligente
- UQ revolutioniert das Geschäft: Von herkömmlichen Unternehmen zu intelligenten Unternehmen

- UQ Rivoluzionando il Business: Dall'Azienda Convenzionale all'Azienda Intelligente
- UQAI Nel Lavoro Remoto: La Nuova Realtà: Bilanciare la Produttività e il Benessere
- UQAI No Trabalho Remoto: Nova Realidade do Trabalho Remoto Equilibrando a Produtividade e o Bem-Estar
- SC Revolucionando Negócios: De la Empresa Convencional a la Empresa Inteligente
- The Power of UQ: The Theory of Balance: UQ (Universal Synchronic Intelligence Quotient)
- The UQ AI Effect: Intelligent Leadership in a VUCA World
- UQ AI: The Key to Intelligent Parameterization in AI
- UQ Course for Visionary Leaders: Lesson 2- Strategies for Implementing ChatUQAI
- UQ course for visionary leaders: Lesson 3 - Valuable advancements with shadows of Plato and Socratic method
- UQ in Artificial Intelligence: Amplifying Success in All Areas of Life
- UQ Revolutionizing Business from Conventional Companies to Intelligent Companies: Universal Synchronic Quotient of Intelligence
- UQAI in Remote Work: The New Reality Balancing Productivity and Well-being
- CURSO UQ PARA LÍDERES VISIONÁRIOS - Aula 3: Avanços Valiosos com Sombras de Platão e Método Socrático
- CURSO UQ PARA LÍDERES VISIONÁRIOS - Aula 5: Solução de Problemas e Autoaperfeiçoamento

- CURSO UQ PARA LÍDERES VISIONÁRIOS - Aula 6: Efeito Girassol na Busca por Padrões e Significados

You can find these works in print version at various bookstores and online retailers, such as Barnes & Noble, Amazon, Goodreads, and ThriftBooks. These works provide an excellent opportunity to delve into your knowledge about UQ balance in different areas of life.

The author also has an author page where you can find more information about her works and stay updated on her latest releases. Take the opportunity to explore these books and immerse yourself in the insights and knowledge provided by author Katia Doria Fonseca Vasconcelos.

www.ingramcontent.com/pod-product-compliance
Lightning Source LLC
Chambersburg PA
CBHW062326290526
45794CB00005B/1914